A Wisconsin Town and Country Christmas

Larry and Renee Lynch

Hedgerow Press
Menomonie, Wisconsin 1987

Copyright © 1987 by Larry and Renee Lynch

Marcia Bowlus illustrations
copyright © 1987 by Marcia Bowlus

All rights reserved.

Published by Hedgerow Press,
1121 12th Street E, Menomonie, Wisconsin 54751.

Printed in the United States of America
by Sentinel Printing, St. Cloud, Minnesota

Distributed by Adventure Publications,
Cambridge, Minnesota 55008

Second Printing 1988

Cover design and art by Marcia Bowlus and Renee Lynch

To
Our parents and grandparents
John and Eleanor Lynch, Rebecca Howerton,
and Richard and Cora Beckmann.

Contents

Author's Note

What was Christmas like when western Wisconsin was still largely covered with pine forests, and towns like Menomonie had only a few hundred souls? When a few hardy farmers were clearing the cutover land stump by stump, acre by acre, a little at a time. When there was no electricity, little money, few places to buy goods. Before Wisconsin was a dairy state, when each farm had only a few cows and raised wheat and oats and barley. When lumber barons built mansions in town and entertained such high society as was to be found on the frontier.

Some folks barely observed Christmas—it was a day pretty much like any other, notable primarily for being in the middle of a harsh Wisconsin winter. Other groups, like the Slovaks and Scandinavians and Germans, brought with them elaborate traditions from the old country, keeping them alive fervently and joyfully, many customs, dishes, and songs surviving to this day.

Although Wisconsin winters in this western hill country were (and are) severe enough to test the mettle of even the hardiest, residents were blessed with some of the most beautiful scenery to be found anywhere, rolling hills primordially covered by vast pineries, later by wheat fields, and then by green expanses of corn that glowed auburn in late afternoons in the fall. In the cold season snow settled over the land, imparting a deep quiet. Dairy farms poked silos and barns through the snow cover, Holsteins repeating the patterns of the landscape.

Settlers came to love this land, as have fortunate residents ever since. We speak from personal experience when we say that it is widely believed in the South that Sun Belt natives could not survive a northern winter, but Wisconsin-ites put on their parkas, scarves, wool-lined gloves, and boots, grab their skis, smile and head for the door. This climate is invigorating, to say the least. Rather than putting a damper on things, cold weather seems to impel people to get out in it, steamy breaths and pink cheeks wrapped around big contented grins.

But enough! Christmas beckons. Father is building a fire in the fireplace, mother is baking strudel in the kitchen, sister is getting out the good dishes, brother is finishing up the chores, and the little ones are playing on the floor.

Early Days

West-central Wisconsin was settled in the wake of logging on such rivers as the St Croix, Chippewa, and Red Cedar. Timber for forts at what is now Prairie du Chien, one of the few eighteenth-century settlements in Wisconsin, is said to have come from the pine forests along the Red Cedar. This river, which flows through present-day Menomonie, joins up with the Chippewa River a mile south of the formerly thriving river town of Dunnville and thence to join the river traffic on the Mississippi.

In the 1820s several lumber mills were built on the Red Cedar or its tributaries in the Menomonie area. In 1846 Captain William Wilson, in partnership with John Holly Knapp II of Fort Madison, Iowa, bought a half interest in a mill owned by David Black. The mill was located on what is now Wilson Creek—a beautiful winding stream with high, wooded banks—just above its confluence with the Red Cedar at the future site of Menomonie. Knapp and Wilson, who gained sole ownership that same year upon the death of Black, were joined by Andrew Tainter in 1850 and Henry L. Stout three years later, creating the lumbering powerhouse that later became famous bearing the bizarre name of The Knapp, Stout and Co. Company. These four giants became the lumber barons of the valley of the Red Cedar. All but Stout ultimately resided in Menomonie and were numbered among its leading citizens.

The village of Menomonie was formally platted in 1859. Its founding is dated by some writers at 1830 and others at 1846, the latter date reflecting Wilson's and Knapp's purchase of the mill on Wilson Creek. It seems that before 1859 thre were few homes in the area. Residents were primarily loggers housed by the lumber company. The first houses were built on the spit of land that lies between the Red Cedar River and Wilson Creek.

In 1861 the Dunn County seat was removed to Menomonie from Dunnville. By Christmas of 1864 an advertisement for real estate placed in the Dunn County *News* claimed a population of five hundred for the village.

The Knapp, Stout lumber company was phenomenally successful, reportedly the largest in the world in the 1870s. It grew rapidly, soon expanding into all manner of enterprises. In 1862 the company boasted saw, flour, and grist mills, steamboats (or "packets") daily plying the Chippewa

River from Eau Claire to Read's Landing on the Mississippi, and a stagecoach line connecting Menomonie with the steamer landing at Dunnville. The company advertised dry goods, saddles and harnesses, woodenware, real estate, groceries, ready-made clothing, drugs and medicines, and everything you could hope for in the way of meat: poultry, ham, venison, bear, and elk.

It took only half a century to harvest all the pine in the Red Cedar valley. In 1901 the last raft floated down the river past Dunnville to the Chippewa, and the great lumber mill was closed. But Knapp, Stout and Company, foreseeing this, began selling its cleared timber land. To promote land sales, the company provided assistance to settlers wishing to farm.

In fact, much of the area was settled by men working for the lumber companies. Throughout the last decades of the nineteenth century, workers would buy up land as it was cleared and begin pulling stumps and sewing crops while still living in town. Then, as the mills closed, they would build a house on the farm land and eventually move out of town, those that had families bringing them to live on the farm.

Waves of immigrants came into the region, the Dutch, the Slovaks, the Scandinavians, the Swiss, the Germans, the Scottish, the English, the Irish. Each poured its own traditions, practices, vocabulary, dress, and cuisine into Wisconsin's melting pot.

Historical Accounts

Written descriptions of Christmas in the latter 1800s are not particularly abundant, but an occasional commentary on winter life and Christmas celebrations in west-central Wisconsin can be found in contemporary letters, diaries, and newspapers.

Some of the earliest accounts of life in Menomonie are contained in the diaries of John Holly Knapp, cofounder of Knapp, Stout and Company. On December 24, 1859, Knapp noted that "many kept this day as their Christmas," and then on December 26 observed that others kept the 26th as Christmas, implying a lack of consensus on the matter. On New Year's Eve of that same season, the thirty-four-year-old Knapp wrote, "The old year goes out quietly & coldly. I have much, very much, to be thankful for. God has truly blessed me during the past year." A few days later he mentions taking a sleigh ride on the river, which was covered by over a foot of ice.

By the next Christmas his thoughts were on the impending Civil War, writing on Christmas Eve of 1860 that "it seems that South Carolina is bent upon seceding from the Union. This is treasonable & if persisted in will break up the Union & involve the whole country in Civil War & perhaps destroy the best form of Government ever devised by Man."

The following year, Knapp took his family sleigh-riding on Christmas morning and reported that "our children are very happy in the enjoyment of a multitude of presents." They celebrated New Year's Eve with a dinner of a "large wild turkey & plenty of oysters." On January 7, 1862, he wrote that "this morning the thickest & most beautiful hoar frost I ever saw covered the trees." The new village of Menomonie evidently had made some social progress by 1863 when Knapp "took tea at Mr. French's where I met several young ladies of intelligence & good appearance, which indicates a good state of society in Menomonie."

The Dunn County *Lumberman*, forerunner of the *News*, ran an amusing item on December 26, 1863. "St. Nicholas is 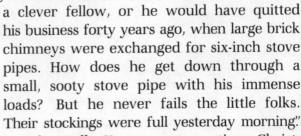 a clever fellow, or he would have quitted his business forty years ago, when large brick chimneys were exchanged for six-inch stove pipes. How does he get down through a small, sooty stove pipe with his immense loads? But he never fails the little folks. Their stockings were full yesterday morning."

John Holly Knapp next mentions Christmas again in 1865, when Captain Wilson and his wife, among others, joined them for Christmas dinner. Throughout these years, Knapp and his family seemed to have gone sleighing for pleasure whenever the weather permitted. On Christmas Eve of 1866 he spent the day getting ready for Christmas and buying presents for the children.

Lou Russell, in *A Gentleman of the Northwoods*, describes a typical Christmas at the John Holly Knapp home overlooking the Red Cedar River. "Garlands of pine bows and lovely red ribbons would adorn every room. Decorated trees would be placed on the large front veranda and a sleigh filled with huge decorated boxes would occupy the front yard." A custom was initiated in Menomonie in 1878 in which ladies willing to receive gentleman callers on New Year's Day with refreshments would advertise in the Dunn County *News*. Ladies of John Holly Knapp's family were among these in 1883.

The Dunn County *News* of December 16, 1871, an-

nounced a "grand Christmas ball "to be held in Cedar Falls, reported that steam heating fixtures had arrived for the new courthouse, and mentioned that the "white bees of winter are swarming in the air as we go to press." On December 23 it contained the odd news that "fifty young widows reside in the small town of Centerville, Indiana, and it is unsafe for an unprotected man to pass through there." Forewarned is forearmed, as they say.

An artist named Jacob Miller was brought to Menomonie in 1857 by William Wilson to decorate his home, and in 1859 Miller bought the first lot and built the first house in the new village of Menomonie south of the lumber mill. Just before Christmas in 1889, Miller wrote in his diary that his wife gave him a dollar to go to town to buy some presents. He bought a bottle of wine, a yard of calico, and some cigars. It's not clear what was later bought with the change.

A merry Christmas

986

Origins of Christmas Customs

Christmas has always been a joyous season but has not always had the form it does now. In the late 1800s and early 1900s there was not nearly the emphasis on gift-giving there is now. Religious observances were the focus in most homes. Some families had exquisite dinners on Christmas Eve or Christmas Day while others had nothing special. Family members often got only one or two gifts or none at all in poorer homes.

But wealth, as everyone knows, does not necessarily bring with it increased happiness. Most people feel that we have lost something in the commercialism now so rampant in this country and even in those countries that contributed traditions still being clung to in pockets and hollows throughout this region and throughout America. "A poignant reminder of the disparity between Christmas as seen through the eyes of an affluent world today and the eyes of a small child in more austere times is found in the reminiscence of Melissa Brown, born in Sauk County in 1861," writes Marilyn Dilly in *Wisconsin Then and Now*. "The Brown family was large and income meagre, but the child Melissa had an explicit faith in Santa Claus. One Christmas morning she remembered arising very early to see if the jolly gentleman had visited and being unable to dress herself in the chilly, dark room. In childish frustration she cried until her mother came in and showed her that the dress's sleeve had been mysteriously sewn shut during the night to hold a large, red apple. 'I was more delighted with that apple than the children of today are with loads of presents. That apple was all I got for Christmas.'"

Anne Short, in an article in *Wisconsin Trails*, notes that "what is now considered a traditional 'old-fashioned' Christmas dates back to the last quarter of the nineteenth century, to the Victorian gilded age. The folkways of Wisconsin's diverse ethnic groups were intermingled then in a rich and colorful holiday pageantry." She notes that nearly everyone adopted the Germans' traditional Christmas tree, as well as the glass balls to hang on the tree, most of which were imported from Germany. Germany also produced the mechanical toys and elegant dolls often received by children at Christmas.

It is clear that songs from many nations have passed into the repertoire drawn on by carolers every Christmas across the country. Everyone knows (or at least knows part of!) such carols as "Silent Night," "O Tannenbaum," and "Away in a Manger" from Germany; "Deck the Hall" from Wales;

"God Rest Ye Merry, Gentlemen," "We Wish You a Merry Christmas," "Jingle Bells," and "Hark! The Herald Angels Sing" from England; "The First Noel," "O Come All Ye Faithful," and 'O Holy Night" from France; and "O Little Town of Bethlehem," "The Christmas Song" (Chestnuts Roasting on an Open Fire), "Joy to the World," and "We Three Kings of Orient Are" from America.

Most of these carols are old, some are new, but they all conjure up "Christmas" as surely as does the smell of pine, of cookies baking, of the turkey when it's nearly ready to come out of the oven, and of scented candles; the sound of bells tinkling and children laughing; the look of snow on the ground and decorations draped across busy, slushy streets and animated figures in store windows and people wrapped up in mufflers and long wool coats and earmuffs and stocking caps.

It is interesting that, according to Rumer Goden, Christmas was not widely celebrated for nearly four hundred years after the birth of Christ. In the early days of Christianity, followers were few and the three great religious observances were Easter, the holiest day of the year; Pentecost; and the Epiphany, which celebrated the coming of the Magi, the miracle at Cana, and Jesus's baptism by John in the Jordan River, which was considered to be His real birth. The

true date of Christ's birth was unknown, and so Christmas was celebrated at various times, ranging from December to January, April, and May.

The 25th of December seems finally to have been adopted, toward the end of the fourth century, because of the proximity of several pagan celebrations, particularly the Roman Feast of Lights, Natalis Invicti, in which bonfires and processions were employed to help the dying sun to be re-born on its weakest day, December 25, the Roman winter solstice. The Norse Yule festival also came in December, the darkest month, when logs were kept burning for twelve days to revive the sun. Portions of two other Roman holidays were also incorporated into Christmas traditions. The Saturnalia, a feast of wild abandon, was celebrated from 17 to 23 December, and during the Kalends, observed on January 1-3, homes were decorated with lights and evergreens, gifts were exchanged, and guests were invited. In addition, the Jewish celebration of Hannukkah, the festival of lights, ends on December 24.

An excellent account of the origins of Christmas traditions may be found in *Christmas, its Carols, Customs and Legends*, compiled by Ruth Heller, from which much of the next few paragraphs is summarized. Caroling may have originated as early as 129 A.D. when Bishop Telesphorus of Rome called for songs to be sung in celebration of Christmas. The word "carol" is from the Italian "carolare," a ring dance from the Middle Ages accompanied by singing. Carols were associated with dancing until the fourteenth century, an activity disapproved of by the church. In England carols nearly died out in the seventeenth century when the Puritans prohibited Christmas celebrations, but they survived as folksongs and were revived in the early nineteenth century.

The creche, or Nativity scene, originated with St Francis of Assisi in an effort to increase understanding and appreciation of the Christmas story. Decorating a tree at Christmas is derived from ancient pagan customs. In Roman times, during the Saturnalia, masks of Bacchus were hung on evergreen trees, and during the sun-worshipping Norsemen's Yule festivities, fir trees were decorated because the growth and blossoming of trees was thought to symbolize the sun. Decorating trees at Christmas seems to have become common in the sixteenth century, probably in Germany.

Placing candles on the tree, before the era of electricity, is persistently associated with Martin Luther, who it is said was out walking on Christmas Eve and, seeing the wintry sky lit by countless stars, cut a small fir, set it up inside the house, and covered it with candles to depict for his family the "starry heaven from which Christ would come."

The tradition of Santa Claus is based on legendary accounts of the life of St Nicholas of Myra, a fourth-century bishop in Asia Minor, who in his youth decided to give away his inheritance. Upon hearing of a man contemplating selling his daughters into slavery because he had no dowry for them, Nicholas dropped three bags of gold through the window, or according to some accounts, down the chimney. One version says one bag rolled into a stocking, originating the custom of filling stockings with gifts at Christmas. The story spread to the Lapps and Samoyeds, where reindeer may have become associated with it. Similarly, the Norse

god, Odin, drove reindeer through the northern midwinter darkness bringing the gift of spring crops. The Dutch brought the story of St Nicholas to America; their name for him, Santa Nikalaus, eventually was transformed into Santa Claus.

The Christmas turkey was an American contribution; in England goose was traditional, and in most of Europe the main fare at Christmas was pig, including ham and boar's head. Many countries had a Christmas cake, and plum pudding was an English tradition.

Living Christmas Traditions and Memories

In researching this book we turned up a wealth of information in books and articles; in old newspapers, letters, and diaries; and, best of all, in interviews with a small cross-section of people representing the ethnic diversity of this part of Wisconsin. All of these people live in Dunn County, but the mix of cultural heritage is typically Wisconsin.

All of those interviewed had lived on a farm at one time or another; a few had recollections extending back into the last years of the nineteenth century, and most remembered the teens and twenties or could draw on stories and traditions handed down from parents, grandparents, and great grandparents.

Nearly everyone remembered having a Christmas tree of some sort, almost universally decorated with candles, and giving and receiving a few gifts (but never very many). Most recalled that a religious service was at the heart of the Christmas celebration. Several people said that a special meal was held either on Christmas Eve or Christmas Day. Those with an English, Irish, Scottish, or Welsh background generally recalled having ham, or stuffed chicken, goose, or turkey, with mashed potatoes and cranberries. The Scandinavians had their *ludefisk* (or *lutefisk*), the Slovaks and Germans their sausage and sauerkraut. Pastries, pies, and breads abounded in these memories, outnumbering nonsweets six or seven to one! Pumpkin, apple, and mince pie; strudel and *kuchen*, *bratzeli*, *kolacki*, *kuchli*, and *fattigman*; plum pudding, cakes, and cookies. A sampler of favorite Christmas heritage recipes will be found at the end of each section in this chapter.

Many folks associated music with Christmases long ago. There was some door-to-door caroling and most people gathered in the parlor or dining room to sing at Christmas. In most communities, visiting with neighbors was common all year long, not just at Christmas. On the other hand, several people said they didn't go anywhere much in the winter—Gladys Nelson of rural Connorsville says it was just too hard to get around. As kids all played ball in the summer and went skiing, sledding, or skating in the winter.

Well, let's hitch up our sleigh for our cultural odyssey back to those simpler days. We arrive at the door on Forest Street for our first stop; the aroma of roast chicken and mashed potatoes and bakery fills the house as our journey begins . . .

Of Plum Puddings and China Dolls, A Scottish Town Christmas, 1895

Christine Granger Klatt, who was born in 1889 and continues to produce historical works from her Menomonie apartment, kindly lent the following manuscript for this book. It recreates a long-ago Christmas in 1895 at her parents' home in Eau Claire, Wisconsin.

On Christmas morning, waking before my sisters, I went quietly downstairs and into the sitting room. There was the tree with what appeared to be white butterflies at the end of each main branch. They were made with white handkerchiefs, folded and tied to the branches with red yarn. Oh! what a sight to greet a six-year-old. It was a family tradition that every member of the clan, except babies, should have a white handkerchief for Christmas—linen ones for the women, cotton ones for the men and children.

Creeping around the tree, I saw a beautiful doll with my name pinned on her dress. The dress was blue with

white lace ruffles at the neck and the bottoms of the sleeves. Her china head seemed to glow. Her white face was highlighted by red cheeks, blue eyes, and short, wavy black hair. Not wanting to be caught peeking, I scurried back to bed, but not to sleep.

After breakfast, with the dishes back in the cupboard, the family gathered in the sitting room to receive their presents. Our father distributed them, to the youngest first and on up to mother and himself. It seemed like hours as I watched my sisters getting their presents. Finally he placed my doll in my arms, saying, "What will you name her?" I answered, "Bessie."

Two days before Christmas, my father had given my sister, Clarissa, and me each a quarter and said, "Now we will go over town so you can buy presents for your mother." My selection was a tray and brush for removing crumbs from the table. The tray resembled a small dust pan, and the brush had black bristles. The brush handle and the tray were red, decorated with gold stars. They were used in my family for many years.

The house at 730 Forest Street was owned by my Grandmother Christina and Grandfather Thomas Wilkie. It was a two-family dwelling. My parents, Charles and Christina Granger, rented the larger apartment and my grandparents lived in the smaller part. All family gatherings were held in my parents' rooms, where there was more space for entertaining guests. The various Wilkies living in Eau Claire continued a tradition started in Scotland, to gather at the home of the head of the clan on Christmas Day. That meant my grandfather's house on Forest Street. Altogether, five families gathered at Christmas.

The preparation of the dinner was shared by the four younger families. The Knutsons brought baked chickens, gravy, and butter because they lived on a farm. The others prepared and brought other dishes. The dinner was served in the Grangers' dining room.

Dessert was plum pudding and my mother always made it. The making of it fascinated me. It was prepared two weeks before Christmas Day and was full of raisins, prunes, and chopped apples bound together with eggs, bread

crumbs, and flour. When thoroughly mixed, it was shaped into a ball, then rolled in flour. A large square cloth was greased and floured in the center, and the pudding placed on it. The sides and corners of the square were tied over the pudding, leaving space for expansion. It was then ready to be put into a deep kettle of boiling water. It boiled slowly for eight or nine hours. When it was taken from the water, it was put into the oven on low heat to dry it somewhat. On Christmas Day it was placed in a steamer and reheated. It was brought to the table ablaze, which seemed wonderful to us children.

My grandfather assumed his rightful role as head of the clan and sat at the head of the table, while grandmother sat at the foot. When grandfather offered thanks, even the children were quiet, with bowed heads and folded hands.

The adults and older boys were seated at the long dining table; the other children ate picnic-style in the sitting room. A large blanket was placed on the carpet, with a table cloth spread over it. The filled plates were brought to the children by the older girls, who helped the younger ones.

After dinner, the men went to my grandparents' quarters to smoke their pipes, while mother and the three aunts were busy doing what was necessary after so big a dinner, chatting all of the time. Grandmother occasionally joined the conversation. When the men returned, the conversation turned to family members still in Scotland: mother's two brothers and a sister.

My Uncle Jim had memorized many of Robert Burns's poems. Sometime during the afternoon he'd be asked to recite some of them. The only words I remember are "for aw' that, and aw' that." None of these Scotsmen ever lost their accent.

Traditional Baked Chicken

chicken   sage, powdered
bread crumbs   onions, chopped

Wash chicken (select roasting hen if possible) thoroughly, inside and out, dry with towel. Prepare old-fashioned dress-
ing of bread crumbs, powdered sage, and chopped onions
moistened with water. Place in chicken cavity, leaving room
for swelling, and sew opening shut. Put bird in medium-hot
oven (in the old days you tested the oven with a hand). After 3-4 hours test bird with a fork in a leg to see if it is
thoroughly baked.

Christine Granger Klatt

Plum Pudding

raisins   brown sugar
currants, dried   cinnamon
prunes, chopped   nutmeg
apples, chopped   allspice
suet, chopped   flour
Scotch whiskey   eggs
                                 bread crumbs

Unfortunately I can't give precise amounts for the ingredients in this recipe since I was little when I watched my
mother make it. I believe it probably was a recipe brought
over from Scotland. When my mother made it, it was to
serve 22 people and the pudding was bigger than a bas-
ketball!

Several weeks before Christmas she cut several loaves

of bread into slices and let them get very dry for bread crumbs. Then a week or two before Christmas she prepared the pudding. She soaked the raisins, currants, prunes, apples, and chopped suet in Scotch whiskey overnight. The cinnamon, nutmeg, allspice, and flour were sifted together in a large wooden bowl, and the brown sugar added. The eggs were beaten by hand and water added to them. All ingredients except the bread crumbs were mixed together. Lastly the bread crumbs were put in the mixture. She knew from experience just how thick the pudding had to be. A large white square cloth was placed on the kitchen table. The center being greased and floured, the pudding was shaped into a ball and placed on it. The four corners and sides of the cloth were tied over the pudding, leaving room for the pudding to swell as it was boiling. A very large, deep, black four-legged iron kettle with a rounded bottom was used. The burner lid from the cookstove was removed and the kettle placed in the hole. Water was brought to a boil, and the cloth-wrapped pudding was put into the kettle and boiled 8-9 hours. Another kettle of hot water was always ready to add to the kettle with the pudding in it. After it was removed from the water, it was put in the oven on low heat to dry the pudding, but not until it was hard.

Early on Christmas Day it was put into a large steamer until thoroughly heated, maybe 2-3 hours, then placed in the oven just long enough to dry the outside of the pudding. It was doused with liquor, possibly Scotch, set ablaze, and brought to the table. Everyone stood up and all said, "Merry Christmas!"

Christine Granger Klatt

Scotch Short Bread

1 cup butter, softened   2-3 cups flour
½ cup sugar   pinch of salt

In large mixer bowl beat sugar and butter till light and fluffy. Add flour, one tablespoon at a time, beating after each addition. Be sure to use butter for it both flavors and makes the bars rich. The dough will be stiff. With hands, make into a ball. Place in center of ungreased jelly roll pan or one similar and push with palm of one hand to spread the dough all over the pan. Make it as even as you can. With fork, pierce the surface. Bake at 250⁰ for about ½ hour. Watch closely the last 15 minutes. Cut into squares or bars while hot.

Christine Granger Klatt

Sour Cream Cookies

Starting when I was 13, in 1902, when our family was living at Dunnville, my duty was to make a batch of these cookies that would last for a week for a family of eight. I've been baking cookies ever since.

2 cups sugar   1 tsp baking soda
1 cup butter, softened   1 tbsp vanilla
3 eggs   5 cups flour
1 cup sour cream   1 tbsp baking powder
                                ½ tsp salt

In mixer beat sugar and butter. Add eggs, one at a time. Mix sour cream, vanilla, and baking soda together. Sift together the flour, baking powder, and salt. Add sour cream and soda mixture alternately with the flour and baking powder mixture. Cover bowl and place in refrigerator over night. Roll out as for any cookie and sprinkle with sugar. Roll lightly, cut with 3" cutter, and bake at 325° for 8-12 minutes. Makes about 125 cookies.

Christine Granger Klatt

Preserving Tradition: The Slovak Settlement

Immigrants from Slovakia arrived in the Boyceville area starting as early as 1890. Slovakia and Bohemia made up the eastern and western parts of what is now Czechoslovakia. The Slovak immigrants were concentrated in an area five miles north of Boyceville that became known as the Slovak settlement. Adele Zavodny still lives on the family farm her great grandfather and grandfather homesteaded nearly a century ago in 1893. John Yamriska, a cousin of Adele Zavodny, now lives with his wife, Annabelle, in Boyceville, but grew up in the Slovak settlement on the same Yamriska farm as Adele Zavodny. Paul Diko was born in Uhrovec, Slovakia, in 1910, moved to Wisconsin in 1929 after three years in Peru, and eventually found his way to Boyceville. His wife, Ann, was born near Boyceville in 1914 and grew up in the Slovak settlement.

Each of their stories added details to a picture of winter life in a Wisconsin Slovak farm community. Even today their recollections of these rich Christmas traditions continue to bring a tear to the eye and a catch to the throat.

On Christmas Eve it was important to "start the chores early" so that the Christmas dinner would not be too late. So the men would feed the cattle and hogs, milk the cows, separate the cream from the milk, and clean the barn, while the women were inside cooking. Perhaps the children would help out with all these tasks, excitement making them impatient for the festivities to begin. Even starting early, they would have to take along a kerosene lantern to the barn as it would be dark before they were through.

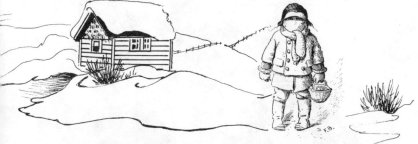

When supper was ready, about six o'clock, all the food would be brought to the table in the kerosene-lit dining room (or possibly in the kitchen) and the family would be seated. Ann Diko said her father would enter from another room carrying two lighted candles and place them on the table. In all Slovak homes, the father would offer a prayer of thanksgiving for the harvest and for all that they had. Then he would ask for a blessing for the coming year, asking the Lord to keep them all well and provide them with good crops. "It was always something special to a little kid, and still is," said Adele Zavodny. Ann Diko added, "It was tradition."

John Yamriska said, "My dad had a tradition. Before the meal he'd go get a little bit of oats, wheat, little bit of corn, whatever he raised on the farm, put it in a bucket, put it under the table. For posterity. He put his billfold on the table for posterity, too. That meant, 'may the good Lord bless the crop and my billfold.' Tradition!"

The father would pour everyone some wine, usually a sweet homemade grape wine. After the family had a sip of the wine, *oplatki* would be served, a bland, paper-thin wafer as big as a pancake and virtually the same as communion wafers. Sometimes a family would sing traditional songs.

The main courses consisted of *lokse*, stale bread cubes marinated in hot milk and water, over which is poured a sauce of honey or sugar, butter, ground poppyseed, and

water; *kapusnica* (sauerkraut and *klobasa* sausage soup); and other dishes, such as *paprikas*, chicken in a delectable gravy served with dumplings (*haluski*) or noodles (*rezance*), and a thick prune soup. Paul Diko, recalling his boyhood in Slovakia, said that his mother made *lokse* one year and *pupacky* the next. *Pupacky*, delicious little round cakes filled with plum jam, sealed, topped with ground poppyseed, and eaten with a fork, were a little harder to make and so weren't served every year. "I preferred the *pupacky*," he said, smiling and licking his lips.

This sumptuous fare would be accompanied by more wine and fruit, nuts, candy, and a rolled bread-like poppy-seed pastry called *roschek*. Nuts in shells were a special treat served only this time of year.

Dessert and coffee completed the feast. Dessert might consist of tissue-paper-thin *strudla* (strudel) containing apples, raisins, and prunes; *fanky*, a rich dough of flour, eggs, and brandy deep-fried like a doughnut and dusted with powdered sugar; and ground-poppyseed *kolacky*.

Adele Zavodny remembers her mother and grandmother doing all kinds of baking at Christmas. Slovak bakery incorporates a lot of poppyseed, which they used to raise themselves. This last summer Adele still found poppies descended from her mother's plants coming up in her garden. Paul Diko explained that grinding the poppyseeds was the secret to releasing their full flavor. Poppyseed was considered a delicacy in Slovakia and was also widely used in neighboring Poland, Romania, Austria, Hungary, and Germany.

A little help with pronunciation? *Oplatki* is "oh-PLAT-key," *lokse* is "LOOK-sheh," *kapusnica* is "kah-poose-NEETS-ah," *paprikas* is "pah-PREE-kahsh," *haluski* is "hah-LOOSH-key," *rezance* is "ray-ZAHN-say," *pupacky* is "poo-PAHTCH-key," *roschek* is "ROHS-check," and *kolacky* is "koh-LAHTCH-key."

If there were time before the church service at eight at the Holy Trinity Slovak Lutheran church, a few gifts would be exchanged. If not, they would wait until after church. The tree, a pine, might be cut ahead of time but not put up until earlier in the day of Christmas Eve. Sometimes the tree would be hung from the rafters with the trunk suspend-ed in a pail of water. In the afternoon it was decorated with candles in little candleholders. The candles would be lit by the father only on Christmas Eve. Generally the only orna-ments were handmade tissue paper roses (John's mother specialized in these) and an ornament made by wrapping a peanut with red, green, and white or silver paper, twisting the ends, and then shredding the "tails" to expose the colors. After Christmas the children would unwrap them and eat the peanuts.

Father would hitch the horses to the sleigh for church. If a family did not have a sleigh they might ride with a neigh-

bor who did. The horses would be covered with blankets to keep them warm while they waited outside the church. There was a Christmas program at church on Christmas Eve that the children participated in. Each child had a part of the Christmas story to recite.

On Christmas morning the children would follow a custom brought over from Europe, which was to go to their neighbors' houses and say their parts; as a reward, they would be given a few coins or a treat.

Slovaks loved to visit, especially around Christmastime, and sing together, traditions that continue to this day. Paul Diko says when they went caroling they always went on

foot. People would put coins or sweets into a container the carolers carried. When families went visiting in the winter they would either walk or ride in a horse-drawn sleigh; they would keep warm by covering themselves with a *perina*, a homemade goosefeather quilt. Women would gather in the winter months to pluck goosefeathers for the quilts while enjoying some pleasant conversation.

Kisla Kapusta
(sauerkraut)

white cabbage, shredded
carraway seed
salt

optional:
horseradish, scraped
beets, whole or halved
apples, whole or halved

In a wooden barrel or a crock put a layer of cabbage, then salt and carraway seed. If desired, add whole horseradish, beets, and apples. Press down with special mallet or other utensil. Repeat layers, pressing after each, until container is almost full. Lay a clean cloth on top of the sauerkraut and put on cover. The sauerkraut will be ready in a couple of weeks. Juice should be skimmed off the top every so often. When ready to use, simmer in pot for a couple of hours (see recipe for *kapusnica*).

Adele Zavodny

Kapusnica
(sauerkraut and sausage soup)

klobasa or *kielbasa* sausage
sauerkraut

dried mushrooms (*huby*)
water

In a pot put sauerkraut, sausage (left whole), and mushrooms. If sauerkraut was made with horseradish, beets, and apples, include them too or add fresh ones if desired. Cover with water and simmer two hours or so. Salt to taste; a dab of sugar is sometimes also added. May be served with potato dumplings (*haluski*)—see recipe below.

Adele Zavodny

Haluski
(potato dumplings)

5 potatoes, grated fine
1 tbsp salt
3 eggs, beaten
3 cups flour

To the grated potatoes add salt, eggs, and flour (enough to make a soft dough). Bring a pot of salted water to a boil. Dip spoon into the boiling water (to prevent sticking) and drop dough by small spoonfuls into the water. Cook 10 minutes, drain, and rinse with hot water. Serve with *kapusnica*, *paprikas*, grated cheese, bacon bits, cottage cheese, or cabbage (see various recipes). This recipe was modified from recipes by Dorothy Kopas in the cookbook compiled by the Holy Trinity Luther League of Boyceville and by Bernadine Wandke in *Wisconsin Slovak*, Christmas 1981, p. 9.

Fried Cabbage for *Haluski*

1 onion, sliced   ½ cup butter
1 head cabbage, shredded

Saute onion in butter until golden brown. Add cabbage and fry until tender, about ½ hour. Add to *haluski* (potato dumplings)—see recipe.

Dorothy Kopas
(Holy Trinity Luther League
cookbook, Boyceville)

Paprikas
(chicken gravy)

2 lbs chicken pieces
(or veal)
¾ cup flour
3 tbsp butter or fat
1 cup water (to start)

1 tsp sweet red paprika
1 cup sweet cream
½ tsp or more salt
1 cup chopped onion

Salt chicken, dredge in flour, and fry on both sides in a heavy iron skillet in butter or fat until lightly browned. Add the onions and cook until brown, then add water and paprika and simmer until meat is tender (45-60 minutes). Pour in sweet cream and warm a few minutes. Serve with *haluski* (dumplings) or *rezance* (noodles); see recipes. Note: you can substitute veal for the chicken.

Julia Jurkovic
(Holy Trinity Luther League
cookbook, Boyceville)

Rezance
(noodles)

4 cups flour
4 eggs

salt
water

Sift flour on bread board (or big bowl). Make a well in the middle. Break eggs into it. Salt and knead to a smooth dough, adding water a tablespoon at a time until pliable but not mushy. Cut dough into several pieces and allow to stand 10-15 minutes. Roll each piece of dough, thin for fine noodles, thick for thicker ones. Allow to dry slightly, then cut in thin strips. (For *sifliky*, or noodle squares, cut noodles ½"-⅓" wide, then crosswise into squares.) Boil in salted boiling water. Cook only what you need; the rest can be stored in a container. Delicious served with *paprikas* (chicken gravy; see recipe) or cabbage.

> Adele Zavodny
> (Holy Trinity Luther League
> cookbook, Boyceville)

Kolacky
(pastry)

9 oz cream cheese
1 cup butter or margarine
2 cups sifted flour
2 tsp baking powder

¼ tsp salt
2 eggs, beaten
prune, apricot, cottage cheese, poppyseed filling, or preserves
2 tbsp sugar

Cream butter and cheese until well blended. Sift flour once, measure, add baking powder, sugar, and salt and work into butter mixture. Add beaten eggs and form a stiff dough. Chill. Roll out ¼" thick, cut with a floured biscuit cutter. Place a spoonful of filling in the center and bake in a 375° oven for 15-18 minutes or until done.

> Janalyn Evan
> (Holy Trinity Luther League
> cookbook, Boyceville)

In a Swiss Valley

Thal means valley in Swiss; Simmenthal means the valley of Switzerland's Simmen River. Katherine Indermuehle's mother and father left the Simmenthal toward the end of the nineteenth century. Katherine lives in an old cheese factory, or, more accurately, in the living quarters of the Annis Creek Cheese Factory, which operated in this valley between Knapp and Boyceville from 1898 until 1960. The Swiss settled in the hills and valleys of Monroe and New Glarus in southwest Wisconsin and in the Knapp-Boyceville area in the west-central part of the state because the region reminded them of Switzerland.

Katherine's mother and father came over from Europe separately, her father in 1884 and her mother in 1887. They married in Menomonie in 1888. Their families had tiny farms in Switzerland, pasturing goats and possibly a few gentle Simmenthal dairy cows with big bells around their necks. Since most farmers had only goats, having any cows made a man a big farmer. Katherine and her son, Ernest Indermuehle, explained that the bells were necessary in the Alps to keep track of the cows.

They left Switzerland seeking better opportunity. Ernest said, "If you were born in the lower class that's exactly where you were going to stay. Not like America. America was the land of promise." Most of the Swiss immigrants to this area came to work for the Knapp, Stout and Com-

pany lumber mill or the railroad, either the Soo Line or the Chicago and Northwestern. About 1890, Katherine's folks started clearing 160 acres of land purchased from the railroad. Her father was still working for the lumber company and the Soo Line at the time, so it took a long time to clear the land. They cut trees, removed the stumps, erected farm buildings, and, with one or two cows and a few horses, sheep, and pigs they gradually began farming. By 1910 they had ten to fifteen cows, a substantial number in an area where most farmers had five or six.

These were self-sufficient dairy farmers, growing wheat

for flour and oats and barley to feed to the cattle and hogs. They separated the small amount of milk produced, taking the cream to the creamery to be made into butter and consuming the skim milk or feeding it to the calves and hogs. When they started making cheese as the century was ending there was whey available to feed to the pigs as well. Ernest said that they made a lot more money on the cheese than on the cream.

In 1898 Katherine's father donated a little less than two acres on the southeast corner of his land for a cooperative cheese factory. He and six other farmers, including his brother, founded the Annis Creek Cheese Factory, the first such factory in this area and one of the earliest in the region (the nearby Tramway and Teegarden factories were built a little later. The Swiss had been cheesemakers in the old country, but cheesemaking was new here.

Katherine, who was born in this Wisconsin valley in 1900, remembers Christmas as very simple, without much fanfare. Her mother baked *kuchli*, a pastry rolled out like a

pie crust, baked in deep fat until lightly brown, and then sugared on top. She said her mother used to bake "washtubs full." Katherine also makes a very thin, flat pastry called *bratzeli*. Ernest asked his mother to get out her special *bratzeli* iron. He said that *bratzeli* was a regional dish in Switzerland not made in Katherine's mother's area. Katherine learned to make *bratzeli* from her husband's family, who were from the Thun area.

The *bratzeli* iron, which somewhat resembles a waffle iron, has designs on both faces that are impressed into the pastry. *Bratzeli* come out much thinner than waffles. Katherine's iron is electric and produces four at once. The older manual ones baked only two at a time in two designs. Ernest said with a smile that "as kids we used to think the flower designs were more tender, better, than the stars, but that's no argument now because the electric iron makes each pastry with a flower on one side and a star on the other."

Katherine says that "where I grew up was very primitive. We were still in the backwoods. Sometimes we went to St John's Lutheran church in Boyceville on Christmas Eve in a sled drawn by two horses. But winters sometimes were severe and we couldn't get to church, so we often celebrated Christmas Eve at home."

She says they sang, had a few treats, and read the Christmas story. They made *kuchli* and maybe had a little homemade grape wine. The Swiss make a wonderful braided bread called *zopfe*.

Although there was no special Christmas dinner menu, "we usually had our own meat on the farm, good beef, always a lot of good homemade soup," Katherine said. "It was beef with vegetables in it, very good. And always milk, butter, cheese, good bread and garden vegetables—we raised our own. We had the beef soup often. The meat was cooked slowly in water, a nice soupbone with meat on it. You gradually added your vegetables when the meat was almost tender, after two or three hours. We added potatoes, onion, carrots, rutabagas if we had them, a little cabbage, just what you had from the garden. Potatoes were one of the main things in it. There wasn't much seasoning needed except for salt and pepper. The beef and the vegetables had the flavor." Katherine still makes soup that way.

She said there were many Swiss families in the valley. They got together all year long, but especially in the winter

they would have gatherings to eat home-cooked food, play cards, argue a little, sing, and yodel!

For Christmas, they would cut a tree but not put much trimming on it; they might hang fruit, apples, and pine cones on the tree, and sometimes the children would make little pictures to hang. Candles on the tree were a tradition attributed to Martin Luther. They burned half on Christmas Eve and the rest on New Year's Eve. Ernest recalled that "as kids we used to let them go out one at a time until the last one had sputtered out. It was a way to see the old year out." There would be singing of traditional Christmas songs, mostly in German, and sledding, tobogganing (in later years), and skiing. Sometimes they would pull toboggans with horses.

Katherine smiled at all the memories, about walking three miles into Boyceville to school, which was conducted in German, about never learning to drive a car. "I'm not sorry about the car," she said with a laugh. "She's got me," Ernest interjected. She paused and concluded, "I have beautiful flowers in the summer, a beautiful yard. I'm very content to be in the country."

Kuchli
(pastry)

9 eggs, good-sized
½ cup sugar
½ cup rich cream
1 tbsp melted butter
1 tsp salt
6 cups flour, well sifted

Beat eggs slightly. Add sugar, cream, and salt. Gradually add flour and beat well to form a smooth batter. The dough is not to be as firm as bread dough, but if it can be kneaded a little that is fine. Chill for an hour or more. When ready to start rolling it out, take a small lump the size of a walnut and roll it out as thin as possible in a round pie crust shape. Make two slits in each and place on napkins to keep until all are finished. Meanwhile, heat lard in a large pot to deep-frying temperature, as for doughnuts. Place one *kuchli* at a time into the hot fat; turn over so that both sides are a nice golden color. I use two long sticks placed in the two slots to turn them and also to take them out. Place baked *kuchli* on large plate and sprinkle with granulated sugar. Store in a covered container.

Katherine Indermuehle

Bratzeli
(pastry)

1 cup granulated sugar	3 eggs
¼ cup brown sugar	1 lemon rind
¾ cup butter	¼ cup milk
¼ tsp salt	3 cups flour

Mix shortening (butter) and sugar, add lemon rind and eggs, one at a time, beating in each one. Mix in milk with one cup of the flour. Gradually add the rest of the flour. Chill the dough until very cold—it can be put into the deep freeze over night. When ready to start baking, take a small amount (less than the size of a walnut) and roll it in your hands into a ball. I usually roll them all before I start baking. This dough needs a Swiss *bratzeli* iron; these used to be manual but now are available electrically heated. When iron is the right temperature, place one ball on each of the compartments and close the iron. Watch carefully as they bake very fast. When baked, I lay them over a rolling pin to give them a nice curve. Some people leave them flat.

Katherine Indermuehle

Zopfe
(Swiss braided bread)

To make one braided loaf:

1 pkg active dry yeast	1 tsp salt
or 1 cake compressed yeast	1 whole egg plus 2 yolks
¼ cup lukewarm water	1 egg white
½ cup lukewarm milk	3 cups unsifted flour
1 tbsp sugar	butter, melted

Add the yeast to the warm water, let stand a few minutes, and stir to dissolve. Add the sugar, salt, egg yolks, and whole egg to the milk. Stir in the dissolved yeast. Beat in the flour. Turn the dough out on heavy floured board and knead until the dough is smooth and elastic. Put the dough into a greased bowl and grease the top. Cover and let rise until double in bulk. Punch the dough down and cut into 3 equal pieces. On a floured board shape each piece of dough into a 14" rope. Put 3 ropes on a greased cookie sheet and braid them as you would hair. Brush the braid with melted butter and let rise until double in bulk. Beat egg white with a tablespoon of water and brush mixture over the risen loaf. Bake loaf in a preheated oven at 375° for 25-30 minutes or until loaf is deeply browned.

Katherine Indermuehle

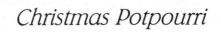

Christmas Potpourri

Paul Holzhueter led the way down into the basement of his Menomonie home, stopped in front of a huge wooden box, and opened the lid. "This was the box my mother brought her clothes across the ocean in," he said. "It took six weeks and she was seasick the whole time." His mother came from Germany at the tender age of eighteen about 1880. His father came over earlier to work for Knapp, Stout and Company, first working in the pinery for one winter and then farming for the lumber company on the Moore farm east of town.

His parents were married about 1887 and moved to their own farm southwest of Menomonie where Paul was born in 1896. There, his family rubbed elbows with the Norwegians to the north and the Pennsylvania Dutch to the west. His former neighbor, Frank Oebser, still lives on a farm in the country. Frank remembers arguing with the Dutch kids about Santa Claus. He says he believed strongly in Santa Claus because his ma and grandma, who raised him, told him stories about the old gentleman with the red suit and reindeer. The Dutch Amish insisted up and down that there was no Santa.

Frank has lived his whole life in the same general

area. His father died when he was little and so he was raised by his mother and grandparents. His mother was born in this country but his father was born in Germany and emigrated with his parents when he was five.

Paul Holzhueter said the strangest thing about Christmas when he was growing up was that they celebrated two Christmases each year, on December 25th and 26th. He said he didn't know why. They would usually go to church on both Christmas Eve and Christmas Day in a sled with two horses; even when they had cars they never drove them in winter. They decorated their tree with candles, popcorn strings, tinsel, a few ornaments, and a picture of Christ on top. There was not a big emphasis on gifts, and mostly only the children received them. He recalled receiving a ten-cent mouth organ and thinking he had gotten a treasure.

On the first Christmas Day, the 25th, the family and maybe some neighbors would gather together for the holiday dinner. They often had smoked pork or ham, sometimes beef, roast chicken, or homemade bologna. The ham was made on the farm, Paul said, soaked in salt water for

six weeks and then cured by smoking slowly in the smokehouse for a week or two. They ate it raw or fried it in its own fat. They cured bacon the same way but it didn't take as long because the salt penetrated quicker.

Sometimes at Christmas they had roast goose and boiled or fried potatoes, home-canned beets, and boiled rice topped with colored sugar sprinkles. There were also, of course, sauerkraut and other vegetables. For dessert they had cinnamon rolls, rosettes, and pie: custard, pumpkin, or apple. He said his mother also made a sort of long cookie or doughnut that she cut a slit in lengthwise. She then pulled one end through the slit to make a knot. Thinking about the butter they had with the meal reminded Paul of how much he used to hate churning butter. It took so long and was hard work! His mother impressed a design on the butter pats with a little wooden mold.

On the second Christmas Day the family would go visiting to the homes of neighbors. Although they did not go caroling, they would sing Christmas songs at home. Frank Oebser also recalls family get-togethers at Christmas, and with all twenty of his cousins in attendance it's no wonder they alternated houses each year. He thinks they celebrated two Christmases "so they could get together a little more," as though they couldn't get their fill of one another in just one day—or the whole rest of the year, for that matter!

Everyone in this area seems to have grown pumpkins to feed the pigs and making pumpkin pie may only have been a side benefit. Frank's family usually had roast goose, duck, or chicken for Christmas but occasionally turkey. They had sauerkraut around all year, including at Christmas, and along with the pumpkin and apple pies and cinnamon rolls they had coffee cake, mince pie, *stollin*, and *kuchen*.

Ray and Lorraine Welch have a farm a few miles to the southeast of Frank Oebser. Ray is of Irish extraction, Lorraine German. Ray is related to the Doane family through his paternal grandmother. Back several generations Sylvester and Sarah Doane migrated from Pulaski, New York, to Plymouth, Wisconsin (near Sheboygan), in 1857 in a covered wagon pulled by a team of oxen. The next year they moved to Dunn County, near Fall City, just east of Ray and Lorraine's farm. That would make the Doanes one of the earliest residents of the Menomonie area.

One Christmas, when Lorraine was about seven, her dad suspected she didn't believe in Santa Claus any more

and decided to teach her a lesson. "I always stayed in and did the dishes before I went out to the barn. When I went out to the barn I heard sleigh bells ringing. I did not know which way to go! My dad had put up some bells on a string and rang them when I started toward the barn. I believed in Santa Claus after that. I can hear those bells just as plain as if it was today."

Lorraine also said that on Christmas Eve after gifts were opened, they would sit around and crack nuts with little hammers on flatirons inverted in their laps. It was a real treat when she was growing up to have nuts in the shell; they didn't have them around except at Christmas. They also both had oyster stew at Christmas time.

There was quite a hill nearby that kids could sled down.

People in their area would go caroling in the horse-drawn sleighs, stopping at farms where folks would invite them in and give them cookies or other treats. They went to church in a horse-drawn sleigh as well. They would heat up what they used to call a "soapstone" in the oven, wrap it in a blanket, and ride with it at their feet to keep warm. Their sleigh was made by the Oscillating Sleigh Co. of Menomonie, quite well known at the time. Lorraine said that if people got cold while they were riding, they would hop out and run along beside the sleigh until they got warm.

Marie Styer, who now lives in Menomonie with her husband, Grant, also remembers running behind the sled when they got cold. Grant and Marie farmed his family farm south of Knapp until 1980, when they retired. Grant was born on the farm in 1912 and lived there for 68 years. He said that when he was a child their Christmas tree usually consisted of a limb that they would cut and stick in a corner next to the fireplace on a bench. They would put lighted candles on it for decoration. "I wonder why we didn't burn the place down," he muses.

Grant's mother was born in Germany, but wouldn't speak German here because "this is America." His father was born in this country, but his grandfather, Loui Styer, was born in Luxembourg and emigrated to America about 1852; his grandmother was Irish. Marie is of English, German, and Austrian extraction.

Neither Grant nor Marie recall a great emphasis on having a Christmas dinner. Grant, raised Catholic, said that the most important thing they did at Christmastime was attend church, though not midnight Mass because of chores. The only special dinner item was pie: "we didn't have pie every day." The pie was either pumpkin or apple, both of which were grown on the farm. In the spring after corn planting, the kids would go out and "poke pumpkin seeds next to the corn hills—our thumbs got kind of sore," he said with a twinkle in his eye. In the fall they would harvest the pumpkins and use some for pie and feed the rest to the pigs, "throwing them over the fence to bust 'em so the pigs could eat."

As with most farmers, they had an apple orchard and grew potatoes, carrots, squash, parsnips, beets, and cabbage.

They had a fifteen-gallon crock of sauerkraut going all the time. Grant remembers that whenever a farmer broke up a new piece of land he would plant turnips the first year and the second year plant a crop. He isn't sure why.

They butchered pork and beef on the farm and smoked ham and made salt pork. His mother used to go out to the smokehouse to cut off some ham for supper from a ham hanging there, which he recalls tasting salty. Beef would be butchered in winter so that the freezing weather would preserve it.

In those days Catholic farm kids were expected to spend two years going to school in Menomonie. They would live with relatives or stay in a boarding house. When Grant was about ten, he and his fourteen-year-old sister stayed in a rented room on 10th St, within walking distance of the school. His sister did the cooking on a cookstove in the room. In the winter when the weather was bad they might not get home for three weeks. But Grant says he didn't get homesick. "I had enough to eat, so why should I get homesick?"

Like Grant, Marie says going to church was important at Christmas. Her whole family always got together for Christmas at the home farm between Downsville and Elmwood, southwest of Menomonie. They usually had roasted chicken rather than turkey, primarily because they raised

chickens, and cranberry sauce. The chicken would be stuffed with a bread stuffing made with egg, sage, onion, milk or chicken broth, and ground-up gizzards, hearts, and livers. They would have mince pie, which she never liked, and blueberry. They grew their own popcorn, from which they made popcorn balls at Christmas by pouring a sugar syrup over the popcorn.

They also made maple syrup, tapping the maples on the property, and put maple sugar in molds to make candy. Every other day they baked eight loaves of fresh bread for the almost half-dozen dinner pails that had to be packed every day. Peanut butter and homemade jelly sandwiches were usual, the jelly made from currants, apples, and plums grown on the farm or from wild raspberries. Every Sunday night, including at Christmas, they would make a cream cake, her dad's favorite, made either with sweet or sour cream and iced with whipped cream or chocolate.

They cut their own Christmas tree, placing it in a jar of

wet sand to support it. They put candles on it but seldom lit them for fear of starting a fire.

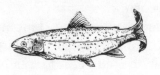

What was that again you said you served for Christmas dinner? *"Ludefisk!"* she exclaimed, grinning wickedly at the interviewer's repeated loss of memory. Anna Peterson was born in 1893 and combines Danish, Norwegian, and Swedish heritage in one neat package. She now lives in Boyceville but spent her early years first near Albert Lea, Minnesota, where she was born, then in northern Minnesota until she was nine or ten, and then on a farm north of Wheeler, Wisconsin. Later, her parents moved near Boyceville so the children could attend high school there.

Anna proceeded to explain about *ludefisk*, about this main dish at Scandinavian Christmas dinners that is codfish soaked in lye, then boiled and served with plenty of melted butter. There may be something inherently hilarious about this dish, since Anna had trouble containing her mirth, though her Slovak neighbor, John Yamriska, who is himself married to a Scandinavian, says *ludefisk* is delicious.

On the other hand, Jill Dean in an article in *Wisconsin Tales and Trails* reports that the dish "is not universally appreciated." She writes that "Swedish children have been known to burst into tears at the prospect of Christmas dinner." Nevertheless, it *is* traditional and the Scandinavians of Boyceville seem to have found more-than-palatable ways to prepare it.

Anna said other typical Christmas dishes were *lefse*, a flat, pancake-like potato bread made with mashed potatoes, flour, and butter, rolled out thin, and baked in a special double griddle or cooked right on top of the cookstove, and *romegrot*, a sort of pudding cooked with cream, milk, flour, butter, and salt. With the *ludefisk* they would usually serve meatballs made of seasoned ground beef. The drippings would be used to make gravy for the mashed potatoes or they might make a milk gravy.

She recounted a special Christmas memory. Her father would come in on Christmas Eve and lie down on the floor near the trimmed tree and the gifts. He would rest his head on a pillow, the children would gather round, and he would sing to them. He would sing traditional Scandinavian songs and the children would sing along.

Ed Evenson, mayor of Boyceville, said the Swedes, Norwegians, and Slovaks in the area intermingled and produced such offspring as "Norvaks" and "Swedaks." He said if you were a recently arrived Norwegian or German settler, "now you got no money, you're broke, so you can't get noplace, you stay right here. So then you write to Norway or Germany, 'here is the heaven's land.' But they told a bit of a white lie—they were having a heck of a time, they weren't making a living. But they wanted to fool the other fella into coming over, they were so lonesome. So more came over and they had to stay too, and that's how this country got built."

He said his Grandfather Evenson was an expert in using dynamite to blast water wells. He also dynamited stumps for farmers clearing their land for crops. Scandinavians had long specialized in blasting and their services were in high demand.

Evenson explained more about Scandinavian Christmas dishes. He said *lutefisk* is more the Swedish spelling, while the Norwegians tend to spell it *ludefisk*. He mentioned several other delicacies, like *flotegrot* (another name for *romegrot*), made from cream and flour and decorated with cinnamon and sugar, and pastries like *sandbakels*, *krumkaker*, and *fatigman* ("poor man"), which is the same as the Slovaks' *fanky*.

Gladys Nelson, who lives on a farm north of Connorsville, traces one side of her family through three Marys and a Marieta to County Cork, Ireland. Her great great grandmother, Marieta Moriarty, died on the voyage over from Ireland; her great great grandfather died before the boat sailed about 1848. They may have emigrated as a result of the Irish potato famine of 1845-48. Her great grandmother, Mary Moriarty, was fourteen or fifteen when she and her sister found themselves orphans in a new land, but they found a good adopted home in Canada. Mary made her way to St Louis, married a railroad man named McGwin, and took in boarders and washing. She told of signs reading, "no Irish and no dogs allowed."

They had a daughter, Mary McGwin, who married a "river rat" named Wall. They lived in Chippewa Falls, Wisconsin, where Wall ran logs down the rivers for the logging company. Around the turn of the century, when the timbering industry was breathing its last, he and Mary did what so many others of the time did, they bought some farm land, below Downing in the "Irish Ridge" area west of Boyceville.

Their daughter was yet another Mary, Mary Wall, Gladys's mother, who married Victor Lewis. They farmed within the village limits of Boyceville, a 200-acre dairy farm with Guernseys, pigs, and chickens. Gladys tended the chickens, gathered eggs, kept the stoves filled with wood, carried water to the milkhouse—but did not work in the

barn because her father "didn't believe in girls in the barn."

Gladys's recollections of Christmas are a blend of Irish traditions from her mother and Welsh traditions from her father. On Christmas Day, they had turkey or sometimes goose with stuffing, mashed potatoes and gravy, and cranberries. There were nuts in the shell and pumpkin pie for dessert. Aunts and uncles came and the older kids that had already left home. The few gifts were placed under a tree decorated with popcorn strings and tinsel and with an angel on top. The decorations smelled good, sandalwood or cinnamon, perhaps. "I can smell it yet," she says. The gifts were all from Santa Claus, and were given out on

Christmas Eve. Gladys got handkerchiefs, which she collected, and dolls or colors or books. One year her sister crocheted her name on an undershirt.

She recalls that her father had a good sleigh with a red velvet seat that was more elegant than the heavy work sleigh used to haul cream to the creamery, but they seldom used it during the long, hard Wisconsin winters.

Our remaining recipes are a mixed bag of German, Scandinavian, and what-have-you. Enjoy!

German Apple *Kuchen*
(coffee cake)

2 eggs	10-12 apples, peeled
½ cup milk	& sliced
2 tsp baking powder	2 cups sugar
1 tsp salt	1 cup flour
½ cup sugar	2 tsp cinnamon
½ cup shortening	½ cup margarine
1 tsp vanilla	

Beat eggs with the milk. Combine next four ingredients and add with shortening and vanilla to milk mixture. Beat with fork until smooth and dough is stiff, about 30 strokes. Spread in a greased 9" x 13" pan. Cover with sliced apples at least 1" thick. Combine 2 cups sugar, 1 cup flour, and cinnamon. Cut in margarine until crumbly. Spread over apples. Bake at 375º for 50-60 minutes or until apples are completely done.

Friedel Lipovsky
(Holy Trinity Luther League
cookbook, Boyceville)

Apple Strudel

1½ cups sifted flour   1 egg
¼ tsp salt   ⅓ cup lukewarm water

Sift flour and salt into mixing bowl. Beat egg slightly with water; add to flour. Mix dough quickly, then toss on floured board and knead thoroughly to make it elastic. Cover dough with a warm bowl and set in warm place while preparing the following filling:

3 tbsp butter, melted   ½ cup seedless raisins
4 cups sour apples,   1 tsp cinnamon
  quartered & sliced thin   1 cup sugar
¼ cup blanched almonds,   ½ cup bread crumbs
  chopped

Lay dough in center of well-floured tablecloth. Roll out a little, brush with melted butter. Put hands under dough, palms down. Pull and stretch the dough gently until 1¼ yards square and paper thin. Do not tear dough. Spread with melted butter, sprinkle with apples, nutmeats, raisins, cinnamon, sugar, bread crumbs, and 3 tbsp melted butter. Hold one end of cloth high with both hands and strudel will roll itself over and over into a large roll. Trim edges. Place in the shape of a crescent in greased jelly roll pan. Bake 30 minutes at 400° and then 15 minutes at 350°. Serve warm with or without whipped cream.

Helen Sokol
(Holy Trinity Luther League
cookbook, Boyceville)

Peffernuisse

1¼ cup dark syrup
¼ cup water
1 cup sugar
½ cup butter
½ cup lard
½ cup walnuts (optional)
2 eggs
1 tsp soda in a little warm
  water
1 tsp cloves
1 tsp cardamon
¼ tsp salt
10 cups flour, approximately

Mix all ingredients together; they are very stiff and hard to mix. Take small amount and roll in long stick. Cut in 1" pieces. Bake on cookie sheet at 350° until brown. They are better if they can be stored for a week or so before you eat them. (This is an old German recipe.)

Marie Styer

Diecher
(potato pancake)

2 eggs
½ small onion, grated
1 tsp salt
2 tbsp flour
¼ tsp baking powder

2 cups grated raw potatoes or
  3 cups cubed potatoes
⅓ cup sour cream
2 tbsp sugar

Original method (using hand-grated potatoes): Mix beaten eggs, salt, flour, and baking powder in small bowl. Add to grated potatoes and pour in greased 9"-square pan or 7" x 11" pan and bake in 350° oven for 30 minutes. Remove from oven and spread sour cream and sugar on top. Return to oven and bake 5 minutes longer. Cut in squares and serve hot;

pour maple syrup over if desired.

New method (cubed potatoes using blender): Put eggs, onion, flour, and salt and ½ cup cubed potatoes in blender and blend until potatoes go through blades. Add remaining potato cubes and continue to process only until potato cubes pass through blades. Use rubber spatula to guide; do not over-blend. Continue as above with original method.

Frances Fruit

Brown Pepper Nuts

1 qt dark Karo syrup
1¼ cup sugar
1 large egg, beaten
1 cup lard
½ cup nuts, chopped

¼ cup sour milk
¼ tsp soda
½ tsp baking powder
9-10 cups flour

Put syrup in large bowl, add sugar and lard, beat. Add egg and sour milk. Sift flour, soda, and baking powder, and add to syrup mixture along with the nuts. Roll in small balls the size of marbles and bake in 350⁰ oven until done and light brown. They are hard and are sometimes soaked in coffee and eaten with a spoon. Or hold in mouth until softened. A half-batch can be made (use a small egg). *Note:* This is another version of *peffernuisse* (see above).

Frances Fruit

Cream Cake with Chocolate Frosting

Sweet cream version:

1 cup sugar
a little vanilla
2 eggs
1½ cups cream

2 tsp baking powder
2-2½ cups flour
whipped cream for frosting

Mix all ingredients, adding flour until batter is medium thick (if cake falls, you needed more flour!). Put in 9" x 12" pan and bake at 350° about 30 minutes until a toothpick inserted comes out clean. Frost with whipped cream and top with sliced bananas. This was my dad's favorite and we had it every Sunday night.

Sour cream version:

1 cup sugar	1½ cups sour cream
a little nutmeg	1 tsp baking powder
2 eggs	1 tsp baking soda

Follow same directions as above. Serve unfrosted or frost with chocolate frosting:

Chocolate frosting:

3 tbsp cream	1 cup sugar	1 tbsp cocoa

Mix ingredients; boil in nonscorch pan. When you lift spoon and the frosting starts to cling to it in strings, it is about done. When cool enough to use, spread on cake. If too thin, add powdered sugar; if too thick, add cream or milk.

Marie Styer

Old-fashioned Sugar Cookies

Sift together:

1½ cups flour	
½ tsp baking powder	½ tsp soda
½ tsp salt	½ cup sugar

Cut in ½ cup butter. Mix all together until resembles coarse meal. Blend in:

1 egg	1 tsp vanilla
2 tbsp milk	1 tsp lemon extract

Roll out on floured board to 1/16" thick. Cut in desired shapes for Christmas. Top with colored sugar before baking (or frost when cold with colored frostings). Bake at 350° until brown, about 8 minutes.

Powdered Sugar Cookie Frosting

2 cups powdered sugar   1-2 tbsp milk
2 tbsp butter   food coloring
1 tsp vanilla

Mix ingredients together; add enough milk to make right consistency for spreading. Spread on cold cookies.

Marie Styer

Floisgrod
(Norwegian milk porridge)

6 tbsp butter   3 cups sweet milk (½ milk &
1 cup flour   ½ whipping cream)
                           pinch of salt

Heat milk until it comes to a boil (or near boil). In separate bowl mix flour, salt, butter, and a little milk until it resembles a white sauce. Add white sauce to hot milk and cook until thick, stirring constantly. For thicker porridge, sift a small amount of flour directly into kettle. Serve hot with butter, sugar, and cinnamon.

Becky Yamriska
(Holy Trinity Luther League
cookbook, Boyceville)

Lefse
(potato bread)

5 cups mashed potatoes	2 tbsp butter or cream
1 tsp salt	2 cups flour

Add butter to potatoes while warm. Let stand until cool. Add flour, working in well. Form into balls and roll into thin rounds. Bake on top of stove or in electric frypan (like pancakes). Spread with butter, sugar, or jam, or slice the *lefse* into 2" x 6" pieces and roll roast beef in it. Delicious! This was from Ma Thompson's kitchen.

Nancy Thompson-Zavodny
(Holy Trinity Luther League
cookbook, Boyceville)

Berline Krans
(Norwegian Christmas cookies)

yolks of 4 hard-boiled eggs	1¾ cup powdered sugar, sifted
1 lb butter	6 cups sifted flour
4 egg yolks, beaten till light	

Slice hard-boiled yolks and cream with butter and sugar. Add beaten yolks and mix well. Add flour. Roll a small amount of dough and shape into a wreath, overlapping ends into a knot. Touch with a dab of beaten egg white where the knot is. Bake at 350º until lightly browned.

Mary Jo Mrdutt
(Holy Trinity Luther League
cookbook, Boyceville)

Epilogue

A few short weeks ago, I was sitting on top of a hill in a half-harvested cornfield in the middle of a beautiful starry night. It was a little chilly, but I could see for miles, the twinkling lights of stars above and farmhouse windows below. I had only recently arrived in this corner of Wisconsin and I certainly never expected to be counting corn gravity wagons at ten p.m. or enjoying it so much.

I wasn't thinking so much as feeling that night, soaking up an incredible amount of friendliness. My wife and I came here almost by accident and without a lot of thought or planning, but here we were. The longer we were here the more something vibrant and exciting entered our lives.

We began this book project a very short time ago. We had no clear notion of why we wanted to do this, but I think I have an answer now. There are so many good people here with such interesting and illuminating stories to tell, living vessels containing all that their parents and grandparents and great grandparents believed in and stood for. And they have not lost the gifts of hope and kindness.

They are not perfect, of course, but they are trusting and generous, and they have changed our lives. I read a wonderful line in an article by Florence Beach Long in *Yarns of Wisconsin*: "Memory is the power to gather roses in winter." The people interviewed for this book dipped into their store of memories and poured out tale after tale, many dredging up information they didn't know they possessed. Repeatedly I sensed that there was something about their contact with the land, with growing things in the ground, tending livestock, and living on farms that may have been in their families for a century that imparted an unexpected depth to their stories. I was amazed at their willingness to share their stories with a stranger coming to the door, sometimes unannounced. And I saw pride in who they are and contentment with their lot in life.

Grant Styer told me, "If you try hard enough, and with some good luck, you will be successful. That is, if you like what you're doing. I tell people I never had to work for a living. It was always a pleasure." Marie Styer regrets that so much of value has been lost with our current hectic, mechanized lifestyle. Despite the hardships in the days before the Rural Electrification Administration brought power to the farms, people got together and popped popcorn, played cards, and talked to while-away an evening. "We're really missing something now," she says.

Ed Wyss, a retired Boyceville farmer, remembers walking to the little country church for the Christmas service. People walked everywhere in those days, often even when horses were available. And they talked and sang and congregated to celebrate holidays and maybe just life in general. Nancy Sorg, who farms with her husband Galen east of Downsville, says there are down times and up times, but the reward is working with her husband; she says it builds a closeness.

Kenneth Larson, a young farmer north of Knapp, summed it up: "I guess I'm just not cut out for city life. I've got thirty-four cows—I don't want any more than that. It's enough to keep the farm rolling. Out here you can make $10,000 less a year and still be happy. It's a good life."

Acknowledgments

This book was assembled using a variety of sources, both primary and secondary, written and oral. Old letters, diaries, and newspapers were consulted as well as books and articles on Christmas traditions and lore and on local history. The heart of the information came from interviews with people living in the breathtakingly beautiful hill country of west-central Wisconsin. Specifically, the author interviewed persons living in or on farms around the towns of Knapp, Boyceville, Connorsville, Downsville, and Menomonie.

Research was conducted in the Area Research Centers/ Archives at the University of Wisconsin Stout and UW-Eau Claire. Especially helpful suggestions, material, and assistance were received from John and Lou Russell, Kay Kruse-Stanton, Fred Flint of the Dunn County *News*, Nancy and Galen Sorg, and Eva Rogers and Frances Fruit of the Dunn County Historical Society's Heritage Center.

Deep thanks go to Grant and Marie Styer, Christine Granger Klatt, Ray and Lorraine Welch, John Yamriska, Anna Peterson, Paul and Ann Diko, Mayor Ed Evenson, Adele Zavodny, Gladys Nelson, Ed Wyss, Katherine Indermuehle, Ernest Indermuehle, Paul Holzhueter, and Frank Oebser for the hours they spent in their living rooms and kitchens reminiscing into a tape recorder and, in some instances, singing, playing violins, twisting and folding paper

Christmas ornaments, digging out old photographs and clippings, and serving up pastries and coffee to a perfect stranger who asked and reasked interminable questions.

Appreciation goes also to the Holy Trinity Luther League of Boyceville for permission to reprint several recipes from their cookbook.

Menomonie artist Marcia Bowlus created several drawings especially for this book, making excursions out into the countryside to capture some of the rural flavor of the area. Her exquisite work speaks for itself. Steve Lampman of Boothby Print Shop helped us all through this project in more ways than we can list. Lori Ausman, Darrell Kauthen, and Dennis Pabich, also of Boothby, were efficient, professional, and above all, very helpful.

I am especially grateful to my son Evan and his friend Christina Pattison, who helped us find sources at the library, and to my wife and coauthor, Renee. She suggested this project in the first place, kept me going when I didn't think we could get it finished in time, and took care of the artwork and layout while I pounded away on the word processor.

Illustration credits: The pen and ink drawings of Dunn County farm scenes on the cover, title page, and on pages 7, 66, and 74 (and the small building on page 35) are the work of Marcia Bowlus (copyright by Marcia Bowlus 1987). The two postcards reproduced on pages 16 and 36 are courtesy of the Dunn County Heritage Center in Menomonie. All remaining illustrations were found in the pages of *St. Nicholas* magazine between the years 1874 and 1909

(Thanks to Linda Cecchini of the University of Wisconsin-Eau Claire library.)

Book and periodical credits: Information on the history of Christmas traditions and carols came from *Christmas, its Carols, Customs and Legends*, compiled and arranged by Ruth Heller (Melville, N.Y.: Schmitt, Hall & McCreary, 1948); *The Reader's Digest Book of Christmas* (The Reader's Digest Association, 1973), especially the section by Rumer Goden; *The International Book of Christmas Carols* by Walter Ehret and George K. Evans (Brattleboro, Vt.: The Stephen Greene Press, 1980); and *The Christmas Book* by Francis X. Weiser (New York: Harcourt, Brace and Co., 1952). For background on Wisconsin ethnic groups and agriculture, the following were consulted: *Wisconsin: A State for All Seasons* edited by Jill Dean and Susan Smith (Madison, Wis.: Wisconsin Tales and Trails, Inc., 1972), pp. 154-56; various issues of *Wiscon-*

sin Tales and Trails and *Wisconsin Trails*; *Side Roads: Excursions into Wisconsin's Past* by Fred L. Holmes (Madison, Wis.: State Historical Society of Wisconsin, 1949); and *Yarns of Wisconsin* edited by Sue McCoy et al (Madison, Wis.: Wisconsin Trails/Tamarack Press, 1978). Historical material on Menomonie and Dunn County came from John Russell and Christine Klatt, and from *The American Sketch Book* by Bella French (La Crosse, Wis.: Sketch Book Company, 1874-75); *History of Dunn County, Wisconsin* by F. Curtiss-Wedge et al (Minneapolis: H. C. Cooper, Jr. & Co., 1925); and *A Gentleman of the Northwoods* by Lou Russell (Menomonie, Wis.: Oak Point Press, 1983). Several recipes were reprinted with permission from a cookbook produced about 1985 by the Luther League of Holy Trinity Lutheran Church of Boyceville, Wisconsin, edited by Marie Zavodny. Some of the recipes were slightly modified for the present book.